LIGHTNING BOLT BOOKS™

How Do Formula One Race Cars Work?

Buffy Silverman

Lerner Publications • Minneapolis

To Jeff, who dreams of zooming!

Lerner Publications Company
A division of Lerner Publishing Group, Inc.
241 First Avenue North
Minneapolis, MN 55401 USA

For reading levels and more information, look up this title at www.lernerbooks.com.

Library of Congress Cataloging-in-Publication Data

The Cataloging-in-Publication Data for *How Do Formula One Race Cars Work?* is on file at the Library of Congress.
ISBN 978-1-4677-9503-6 (lib. bdg.)
ISBN 978-1-4677-9681-1 (pbk.)
ISBN 978-1-4677-9682-8 (EB pdf)

Manufactured in the United States of America
1 – BP – 12/31/15

Table of Contents

Built for Speed

Formula One race cars zip around a racetrack. Engines roar. Four wheels stick out from the sides of the cars. Their large tires grip the track.

A formula is a set of rules. Formula One cars and drivers follow the same rules.

A Formula One car has only one seat inside. The driver sits in the cockpit.

This is the body of a Formula One car.

The outside part of the car is the body. The body is made from one piece of material. It is strong and light. It is built for speed!

Air flows around a moving car. Air pushing against a car slows the car down. Formula One cars are shaped to slip through air more easily.

Air that slows a car is called drag.

Formula One cars are tested in wind tunnels. Wind tunnels show which parts of a car create the most drag.

Air flows around a car in a wind tunnel.

Start Your Engines!

The engine of a Formula One car is behind the cockpit. The engine changes fuel into energy that makes the car move.

Pistons move inside an engine. When a piston goes down, it pulls air and fuel into a chamber. Then the piston slides up and squeezes the air and fuel. A spark burns the fuel and pushes the piston back down.

Pistons move up and down.

Pistons turn a crankshaft when they go up and down. The pistons and the crankshaft make the race car's wheels turn.

The crankshaft spins when the pistons move.

The crankshaft in a Formula One engine spins much faster than the crankshaft in your family's car. This helps Formula One cars zip around the track. They can go faster than 200 miles (322 kilometers) per hour!

When a powerful engine runs, it makes a lot of heat. Some of that heat is turned into energy to help the car zoom!

Too much heat harms an engine. Mechanics must repair and rebuild it.

On the Track

The tires on a Formula One car are wide and lightweight. The soft rubber of the tires grips the road.

Soft rubber wears out quickly. Formula One tires must be changed often.

This tire needs to be changed.

A team changes tires at the pit. The team can change all four of a car's tires in less than three seconds.

The wings on a car help it grip the road. A Formula One car has wings on the front and the back.

This is a Formula One car's front wing.

Air flows over and under the wings. The wings are shaped so that air flows faster under the bottoms of the wings than over the tops. Slower-moving air pushes down on the tops of wings. The air and the wings make a downforce.

Do you see the wings on this Formula One car?

Downforce helps tires grip the road. Lightweight Formula One cars need downforce from wings to stay close to the ground. But large wings add drag and slow a car.

Workers change the angle of the back wing. They increase or decrease the downforce and the drag.

The angle of this wing can change.

Staying Safe

What happens if there is a crash? A helmet and special clothes help to keep a driver safe. A suit protects a driver from fire.

A driver slows a car as he nears a turn in the track. He steps on the brake pedal. Brake pads press against discs on the wheels. The wheels turn more slowly.

This is a disc on a Formula One car's wheel.

Look out! If a driver brakes too quickly, a car can skid off the track. **Drivers learn to slow down safely.**

A Formula One car slides off the track and crashes.

Rub your hands together. You feel heat. The heat is from friction. Friction occurs when two things rub against each other. A car's brake pads and discs create a lot of friction. They make heat.

If brake pads and discs get too hot, they don't work well. Special ducts bring air over the brake parts to cool them.

Ducts behind this plastic help cool a Formula One car's brakes.

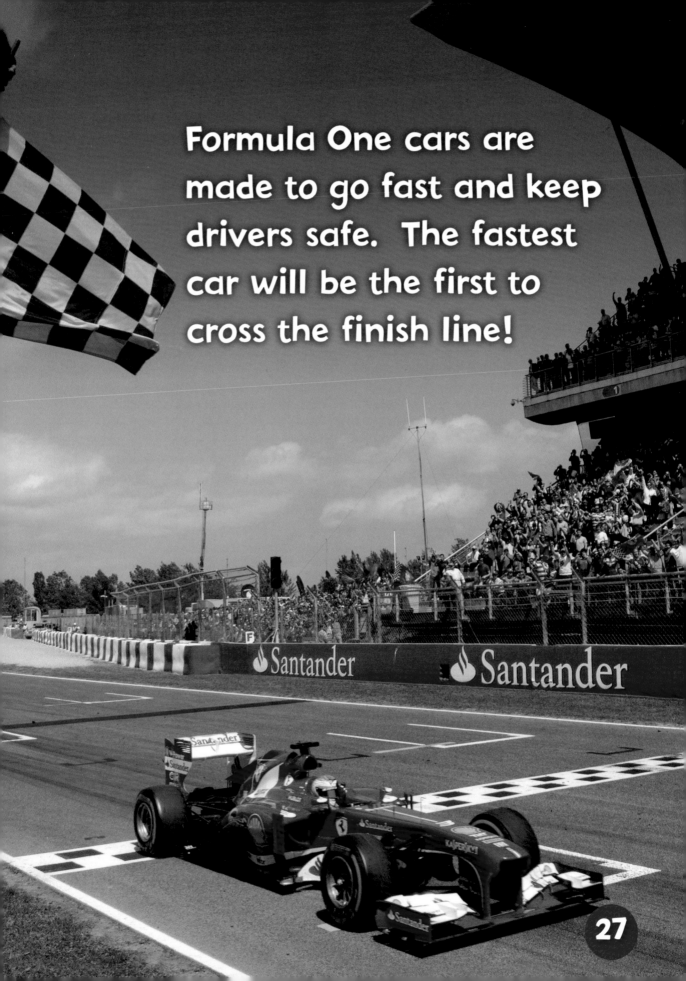

Formula One cars are made to go fast and keep drivers safe. The fastest car will be the first to cross the finish line!

Diagram

wing

cockpit

body

DRAG

engine

tire

wing

Formula One Race Car

Fun Facts

- The top speed ever recorded for a Formula One car was 247 miles (397 km) per hour. In 2006, the record was set at Utah's Bonneville Salt Flats.

- Modern Formula One engines are less powerful than they were in the 1980s. But modern race cars still go just as fast, because they create less drag than they used to.

- Most Formula One races are on tracks called circuits. The Monaco Grand Prix in Europe runs on a circuit laid out on city streets.

Glossary

cockpit: the place where the driver sits in a Formula One car

crankshaft: a long piece of metal that connects a car's wheels to its engine

disc: a metal plate that is mounted to the wheels and squeezed by pads to slow a car

downforce: a force that presses a car down

drag: the force of air that slows a moving car

duct: a channel that air flows through

engine: a machine that gives a car power to move

friction: the rubbing of the surface of one thing against another

piston: a part of an engine that moves up and down and makes other parts move

pit: an area next to the track where a driver can stop to get gas, change tires, and make repairs

Further Reading

Car Friction: The Science of
Going Fast
http://www.education.com/science-fair/article
/car-friction/

DragonflyTV — Wind Tunnel
http://pbskids.org/dragonflytv/show/windtunnel.html

Filipek, Steele. *Race Car Drivers: Start Your
Engines!* New York: Grosset & Dunlap, 2009.

Sutherland, Adam. *Being a Formula One Driver.*
Minneapolis: Lerner Publications, 2013.

Zemlicka, Shannon. *From Iron to Car.* Minneapolis:
Lerner Publications, 2013.

Index

Photo Acknowledgments

The images in this book are used with the permission of: © Clive Mason/Getty Images, pp. 2, 4, 13; © Getty Images for Grand Prix Masters, p. 5; REUTERS/Thomas Peter, p. 6; © Darrell Ingham/Getty Images, p. 7; © Allsport UK/Getty Images, p. 8; © Franck Fife/AFP/Getty Images, p. 9; © Krasowit/Shutterstock.com, p. 10; © Maruo1969/Shutterstock.com, p. 11; © Johannes Eisele/AFP/Getty Images, p. 12; © Hans Neleman/Getty Images, p. 14; AP Photo/Thomas Kienzle, p. 15; © Tom Gandolfini/AFP/Getty Images, p. 16; © Jewel Samad/AFP/Getty Images, p. 17; © Clive Rose/Getty Images, p. 18; © Charles Coates/Getty Images, p. 19; © Stan Honda/AFP/Getty Images, p. 20; © Rainer W. Schlegelmilch/Getty Images, p. 21; © Mark Thompson/Getty Images, p. 22; © Sutton Images/Corbis, p. 23, 26; © Jim Watson/AFP/Getty Images, p. 24; AP Photo/Michael Probst, p. 25; © Tom Gandolfini/AFP/Getty Images, p. 27; © Laura Westlund/Independent Picture Service, p. 28; © Handout/Getty Images, p. 29; © pilipus/Alamy, p. 31.

Front cover: © viledevil/Deposit Photos.

Main body text set in Johann Light 30/36.